⇒ WELCOME TO ⇒
PICKER'S
PARADISE

10 SECRETS TO BECOMING A JUNK LOVIN', DEAL SEEKING PICKER

JP BENTLEY

Library of Congress Cataloging-in-Publication Data is available.

ISBN 978-0-9855947-0-1

Sheltie Press
2043 Vista Cajon
Newport Beach, CA 92660

www.Sheltiepress.com
info@Sheltiepress.com

Printed in the United States of America

First Printing May 2012

10 9 8 7 6 5 4 3 2 1

For Spencer and Dani --
future pickers of America

shion Sense

a Haystack

of the Deal

la One Dolla

Bird Gets the

Ming Vase?

Cool Man

Battles

Reward

to Score

1.Pi

Fas

Se

cker

hion

nse

Stealth is a good look for you

Being a picker is like being a deer in the hunt - you don't want to stand out and get picked off. Sellers are looking for easy prey to push up the costs on cheap items. When a seller sees you coming wearing expensive clothes or jewelry, the price of that guitar just went from $40 to $80.

No

Yes

Look the part

In the world of swap meets and garage sales, image is not your friend. Comfort is king. Don't clean those pair of sneakers and don't be afraid to wear the shirt you wore to bed. Be prepared for weather changes by layering your clothing. Bring a sweater in case Mother Nature decides to take a chill pill. The more you blend in, the better. Picker fashion is the first key to successful buying.

"I dress to kill, but tastefully."
-- Freddie Mercury

Must haves

Large sunglasses with dark lenses
To shield the seller from noticing your
pupils dilating from excitement.

Comfy sneakers - Avoid unneeded
stress on your legs and prevent those
pesky varicose veins

Hat - Large brimmed is preferred,
but anything will do in the hot sun.

Fanny pack -Filled with plenty
of dollar bills

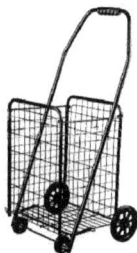

Pull cart- gotta carry that rusty gold.

Hand Sanitizer - To feel 'clean'
after a hard day of picking

2.Ne in Hays

edle

a

tack

A treasure is in there somewhere

Nothing is more rewarding than finding something special and valuable while picking. This is why we do what we do. It is the nirvana of junk. But finding that treasure is rarely as easy as the tv shows make it seem.

Take a few deep breaths as you enter that garage sale driveway or swap meet vendor booth. Do not let yourself get over-whelmed by the amount of items staring back at you. Turn your picker scanner on in your brain and become one with the junk.

Find
your
inner
picker

Begin your search process slowly, keeping in mind that there are other garage sales and tables to get to in a timely manner. Focus on looking for that unique item that stands out to you. Most garage sales, swap meets and thrift stores have a hodge-podge of items in no particular grouping. Your treasure can be found in a bucket of used dog chews. In other words - keep an open mind during your hunt and find that needle!

"What you gon' do with all that junk?
All that junk inside that trunk?"
— Black Eyed Peas

We interrupt this book to give you a very important reminder to use the following essential tool at your immediate disposal:

Before buying any item, use your nose. If you smell smoke, urine or substances of an unknown nature - drop it! Even the cutest little stuffed bear can become a real bear.

This has been a public common sense message from us pickers who care.

WARNING
TOXIC TEDDY

3.The
of
de

art
the
al

Picasso of picking

Getting a great deal is an art in itself. It takes patience and a good sense of reading people. Be polite, smile and don't bite. A seller is there to sell. It is that simple. You are the conduit for money in the seller's pocket. Make it easy for the seller to accept your money. This is a delicate dance that requires balance. Keep the transaction as simple and pleasant as possible.

Do not go there

#1. Don't...pull out a wad of $20 bills for the world to see before asking the price.

#2. Don't.....talk about how 'awesome' the item is and how it reminds you of your mother's kind smile.

#3. Don't.....throw or toss an item back. The seller got up at the crack of dawn to arrange those items on that table to make it look 'just right'.

#4. Don't.....insult the seller with a gasp of disbelief and horror in response to a verbal price.

the path to the deal

Step 1
Casually pick it up and
inspect it

Step 3
Make eye contact with
the seller

Step 2
Discreetly reach into your
fanny pack and pull out the
exact amount you are
willing to pay

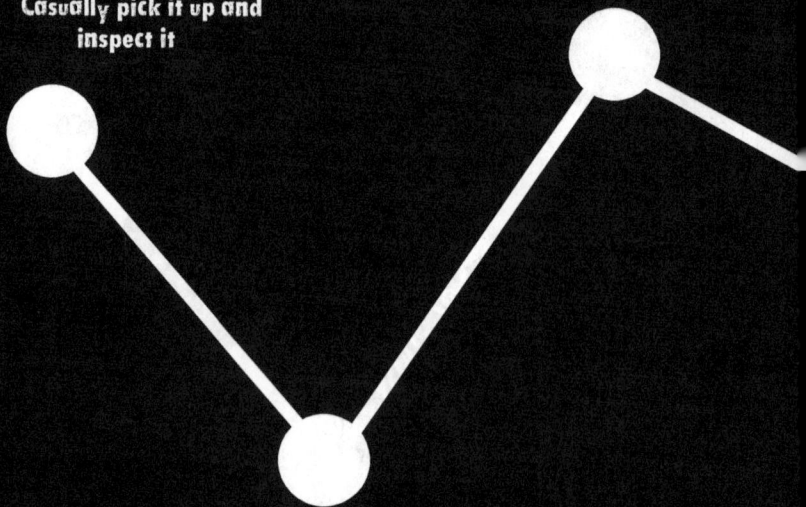

Step 6
Stretch out your arm with the dollar bills cascading out of your fingers and in a firm voice offer the amount you have. In other words SHOW HIM DA MONEY!!!

Step 4
Hold up the item and in a calm, semi uninterested voice ask how much

Step 5
If the amount is too high, point out the chipped paint and any conceivable defect you can find on this item

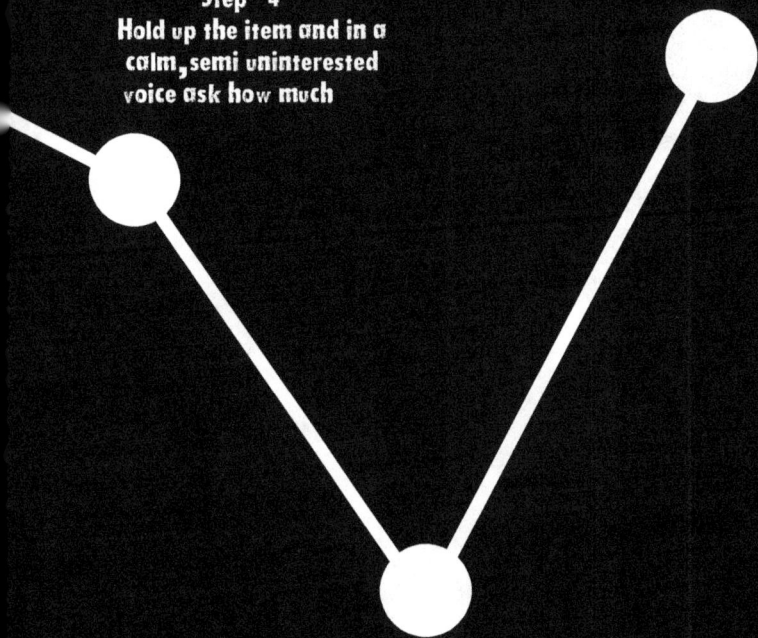

4. One
One

dolla

dolla

George is your man

As a picker, it is no secret that cash is king. You need to have ample change when arriving at any sale or swap meet. Your debit card most likely won't be useful at your local garage sale. It is a good idea to get small change the day before shopping. Flashing $100 bills may impress your friends, but most sellers prefer smaller denominations. If the item you are purchasing is $22 and you only have a $100 bill on you, the item might escape you if the seller doesn't have exact change. Make your life easy and be prepared.

"One dolla, one dolla" being yelled from a swap meet vendor. Check it out! Many treasures can be found at the dollar tables.

Bring money in the form of dollar bills. Throw in some fives and maybe a few tens, but make sure you have plenty of dollar bills. This will give you more leverage by having exact change and for quick bargaining power.

"I'm an ocean, because I'm really deep. If you search deep enough you can find rare exotic treasures."
— Christina Aguilera

5.The early gets

bird
the...

What time is it?

Sleep in on Saturdays? You can kiss that goodbye. There is a lot of competition out there with lots of roomy space in their vans, so if you want to play with the big dogs, GET UP EARLY!!!!

Tip: Set your alarm for around 6am if you have a late Friday night where your Aunt Sally forces you to view her slideshow from her 1974 trip to the Grand Canyon.

"Early to bed and early to rise makes a man healthy, wealthy and wise".
— Benjamin Franklin

6:30am Score!

Typical Saturday morning

- Wake up your lazy butt
- Get your coffee and toaster tart
- Slip on comfortable pants
- Wear the t-shirt you slept in
- Slather on some sunscreen
- Grab a hat
- Get your cart if you are hitting the swap meet
- Have garage/estate sale addresses handy
- Confirm you have your cell phone
- Pack your fanny pack or wallet with plenty of dollar bills
- Place cushy shoes on your feet
- Head out the front door to begin your treasure hunt

6.

Is th

Ming

at a

vase?

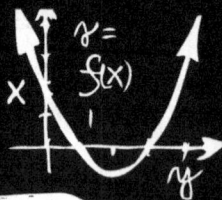

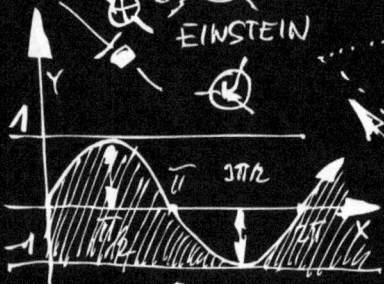

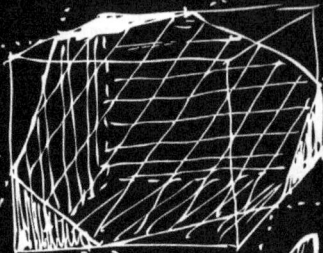

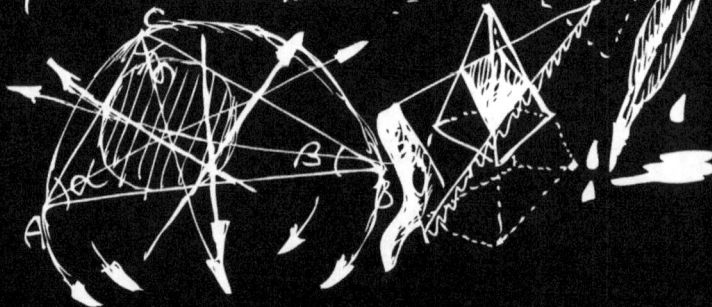

A PHD in picking

You don't need to memorize the collectible encyclopedia to begin your picking journey. The process of buying and selling items is the most valuable education. You will inevitably pay too much for certain items. You will score incredible deals on other purchases. Experience is your best tool in becoming a successful picker. Whether you stay consistent with the items you purchase or prefer to mix it up, your degree of knowledge will grow in relation to the amount of items you buy and sell. Don't over-think it and remember to have fun!

Rookies lose

The chances of finding treasures during your picking adventures are high. The chances of finding a Ming Dynasty vase worth a gazillion bucks is a long shot. Don't decide to be a picker with the expectation of finding the lost treasure. Don't get discouraged when you find your picking buys for the day didn't render a humongous profit. Like anything in life, the more you practice, the better the results (with the exception of professional head-butting).

"Learning is a treasure that will follow
its owner everywhere."
— Chinese Proverbs

Rookie Mistake: Wow, a cool vintage toy. What a score!
Reality: The year 2009 is printed on the bottom of the toy.

Rookie Mistake: Wow, this book is really old so it must be worth a fortune!
Reality: The value of a book is determined by the number printed of that particular edition. Don't assume that because an item is old, it is valuable.

7.Pla
cool

y it
man

I had no idea

There is nothing more exciting than spotting a treasure on the garage sale table in front of you. While it can be hard to contain your excitement, it will behoove you to stay calm and casually ask the seller for a price. It isn't a good idea to ask "How much for this rare, highly sought-after collectible figurine?" You will purchase many items along your picking journey that you won't know the value of until after you purchase it. When you do spot that treasure you have been waiting to purchase, resist the urge to grab it and scream "This is mine!" Play dumb and score a great deal.

Buyer Tip:

Cameras are a great buy if you can get it for the right price.

"Don't you understand,
your brain is clay and I
gotta squeeze it!
— The Fonz

You are holding a circa 1900's Tiffany lamp in your hands. Play it cool, man. Grab a small bouncy ball to go along with the lamp and offer $10. Don't let the seller think you have any idea what you are holding. A perfect comment to use at this point would be something along the line of "This will go great in my daughter's room." This is the one industry where playing dumb is smart!

8.

Pick bat

your

tles

Just walk away

Knowing when to fold your cards and walk away from a deal is an important skill. It is easy to get caught up in the excitement of the haggle. You can get as close as a few dollars apart in price, but if you aren't going to make the profit you need, put it down and move on to other items. There are sellers that place a higher value on certain items that may hold a special place in their heart. Pick your battles.

Deal scenario

You spot that vintage belt buckle that you know you can make a profit on if the price is right. You ask the seller for a price. Your arm hair stands on end while beads of sweat form on your eyebrows. You hear the seconds ticking in your head. The moment of truth comes when the seller comes at you with... retail price. Your heart drops to your underwear wedging in your butt crack. You pull out dollar bills and point out the scratches on the belt buckle. You offer your price. If the seller doesn't budge, just walk away. Face it, you are not going to get a deal on everything.

Actual picture of J. Bentley (bad hair day) with a belt buckle he
bought at the $1 table and later sold for $49.99.

Mobile apps= success

You are not going to be able to check the fair buying price of every item using your mobile app before purchasing. However, if the circumstances allow (and without looking like an obvious picker) take the time if you are unsure about the seller's price to walk away and use your mobile device to check the price online. This will ensure that you don't get home and realize you were hosed on the price.

Check, check, check
- Always have your phone ready in hand
- Make sure you have an app or a search engine ready
- Be discreet about your approach to checking

CHECK ME OUT BEFORE YOU BUY ANYTHING

9.
Sunn
of pi

y side

cking

The following over-used catch phrases
apply to the advantages of being a picker:

Be your own boss
Work from your home
Make thousands a month (it's possible)
No office environment
Save money on your wardrobe
Work outside

do what you love to do

Being a picker is not only fun and exciting, it is a way of life. You are out in the fresh air, interacting with people from all walks of life while looking for that next treasure. It is a passion in you. The desire to find that next great antique hiding in that bin under the neighbor's garage sale table. There are many reasons to love being a picker, but you already know this. Now go out and enjoy the hunt!

True case from the Picker Files

In 2010, a commercial painter learned that two boxes of glass photo plates he paid $45 dollars for at a garage sale was estimated to be worth more than $200 million. They turned out to be original Ansel Adams negatives in the plates.

"Happiness is your own treasure because it lies within you."
--Prem Rawat

have fun with it

Give yourself a picker nickname:

Bundling Bob - Always bundles a minimum of two items in his hand before asking for a price

Low-ball Larry - Offers $1 for that working flat screen TV

Flirting Fanny - adds a hug at the end of every deal

Hippy Harry - very casual with cash in bell bottom pant pocket.

10.
Getr
to sc

eady
ore

pickers list

Appropriate attire – blend in
Comfy tennis shoes
Sunscreen and hat
Be prepared with lots-o-dollar bills
Get up and at ' em early
mobile device to check prices
Buy Low – Sell High – {Duh}
Be nice

Plan before you pick

When planning on hitting garage and estate
sales, take the time the night before and check
out the online classified listings and your local
newspaper. Map out the garage and estate sales
by location. This will save on time and gas.

"I saw this movie about a bus that had to
SPEED around a city, keeping its SPEED over
fifty, and if its SPEED dropped, it would
explode! I think it was called, 'The Bus That
couldn't Slow Down."
--Homer Simpson

Yet another true case from the Picker Files

In 1989, a man from Philadelphia bought a $4 painting at a garage sale, found an original copy of the Declaration of Independence inside, and sold it for $2.4 million. Wow.

where to go

Swap Meets

Garage Sales

Thrift Stores

Auctions

Large Trash Bins

Moms house

Never
the wee
almost

fear,
kend is
here.

Thank you

We thank our incredible children Spencer and Dani - who are our inspiration for all that is great in this world.

We are thankful for our fellow pickers who share our love for the hunt for treasure.

To our supportive family and friends who know better than to invite us to any activities on a weekend morning.